The Co...

Compiled by Lynn Purdie
Designed by Sam Macnamara

PBR

A Pillar Box Red Publication

© 2011. Published by
Pillar Box Red Publishing Ltd.

Photography © Shutterstock.com
ISBN: 978-1-907823-20-6

£7.99

CONTENTS

Animal Ha Ha

1 Why did the kangaroo go to the hospital?
Because he needed a hoperation!

2 What do you give a sick pig?
Oinkment!

3 What is the difference between a flea and a wolf?
One prowls on the hairy and the other howls on the prairie!

4 Why did the bee go to the hospital?
Because he had hives!

5 What's small and cuddly and bright purple?
A koala holding his breath!

6 What do you get if you cross a teddy bear with a pig?
A teddy boar!

7 What happens when a cat eats a lemon?
It becomes a sour puss!

8 What do you get if you cross a fish with an elephant?
Swimming trunks!

9 What do mice do when they're at home?
Mousework!

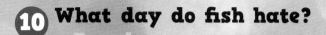

10 What day do fish hate?
Fry-day!

11 What do call a bear with no ears?
B!

12 Why is it hard to play cards in the jungle?
There are too many cheetahs!

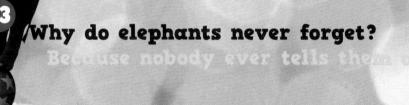

13 Why do elephants never forget?
Because nobody ever tells them anything!

14 What do you get when you cross a parrot with a centipede?
A walkie talkie!

What is a crocodile's favorite game?
15 Snap!

16 What happens when a frog's car breaks down?
He gets toad away!

Answers on page 60.

SPOT THE DIFFERENCE

Can you help Hardy Har to find the 6 differences between the photographs?

I'm a bit stuck

YOUR FAVOURITE FUNNIES

Who is the best dancer at the Monster Ball?
- The Boogie man. (Brennan, age 6).

Where do cows go on holiday?
- Moo York! (Megan, age 6).

What does a frog drink?
- Croak a Cola! (Casey, age 5).

What did the baby light bulb say to the mamma light bulb?
- I love you watts and watts! (Erica, age 9).

How many rotten eggs does it take to make a stink bomb?
- A phew! (Euan, age 6).

YOUR FAVOURITE FUNNIES

What does the word minimum mean?
- A small mum! (Joe, age 8).

Why did the horse cross the road?
- To visit his neiiiiiiighbours! (Luca, age 6).

What do you call a fly with no wings?
- A walk! (Chelsea, age 6).

Why does a French man only have one egg at breakfast?
- Because one egg is un oeuf! (Lily, age 7).

What do you call a blind dinosaur?
- Do-you-think-he-saur-us! (Mia, age 5).

Why did Mickey Mouse take a trip into space?
- He wanted to find Pluto! (Brandon, age 5).

KNOCK
KNOCK

Knock Knock
Who's there?
Abe!
Abe who?
Abe C D E F G H...!

Knock Knock
Who's there?
Big ish
Big ish who?
No thanks!

Knock Knock
Who's there?
Cargo!
Cargo who?
Cargo better if you fill it with gas first!

Knock Knock
Who's there?
Dancer!
Dancer who?
Dancer is simple, it's me!

Knock Knock
Who's there?
Earwig!
Earwig who?
Earwigo, Earwigo, Earwigo!

Knock Knock
Who's there?
Fido!
Fido who?
Fido known you were coming I'd have left the door open!

Knock Knock
Who's there?
Gopher!
Gopher who?
Gopher help -I'm stuck in the mud!

Knock Knock
Who's there?
Hatch!
Hatch who?
Bless you!

Knock Knock
Who's there?
Ivor!
Ivor who?
Ivor good mind not to tell you now!

Knock Knock
Who's there?
Jim!
Jim who?
Jim mind if we come in?

Knock Knock
Who's there?
Ken!
Ken who?
Ken you let me in?

Knock Knock
Who's there?
Lass!
Lass who?
That's what cowboys use, isn't it?

Knock Knock
Who's there?
Mabel!
Mabel who?
Mabel doesn't ring either!

13

```
G P E L T R T K H P P D W T
N C L H L G A G D L R Z F F
I R K K S C R E A M A Z C H
T A C F L M G C Q M C K M I
T Z U B N W I E K W T F F L
I Y H D F T L G L D I Y J A
L K C T N G T Y F J C G Z R
P H X A G Z K W L H A J T I
S G Q I F I B J I L L R R O
E U G M D U O Q X I N N U
D A G D Y K N R D R D S D S
I L I G E V H N Y N T U L C
S N R N Z L Q J Y B D H P P
G Q N K N A R P J D T C K N
```

Answers on page 60.

14

SEARCH

All of the words below are mixed up in the wordsearch grid. The words can go horizontally, vertically or diagonally in any direction.

Antic	Kidding
Chuckle	Laugh
Crazy	Practical
Funny	Prank
Gag	Scream
Giggle	Sidesplitting
Hilarious	Silly
Joke	Windup

Our little EggHead isn't sure he can solve the wordsearch. Can you do any better?

Family Fnar Fnars

Brother: "If you broke your arm in two places, what would you do?"
Sister: "I wouldn't go back to those two places, that's for sure."

Peter: "What position does your brother play in the school football team?"
Susie: "I think he's one of the drawbacks!"

Big Brother: "That planet over there is Mars."
Little Brother: "And is the other one Pa's?"

What do you call two people who embarrass you in front of your friends?
Mum and Dad!

Little girl: "Daddy, Daddy, can I have another glass of water please?"
Dad: "But I've given you 10 glasses of water already!"
Little Girl: "Yes, but my bedroom is still on fire!"

What did the father ghost say to the naughty baby ghost?
"Spook when you're spoken to!"

Family Fnar Fnars

One evening a little girl and her parents were sitting around the table eating supper.
The little girl said, "Daddy, you're the boss, aren't you?"
Her daddy smiled, pleased, and said yes.
The little girl continued, "That's because Mummy put you in charge, right?"

There was this little kid who had a bad habit of sucking his thumb. His mother finally told him that if he didn't stop sucking his thumb, he'd get fat. Two weeks later, his mother had her friends over for a game of bridge. The boy pointed to an obviously pregnant woman and said, "Ah, ha! I know what you've been doing!"

"What's your father's occupation?" asked the school secretary on the first day of the new academic year.
"He's a conjurer Miss," said the new boy.
"How interesting. What's his favourite trick?"
"He saws people in half."
"Gosh! Now, next question. Any brothers or sisters?"
"One half brother and two half sisters."

My sister is so dim she thinks that a cartoon is a song you sing in a car!

Mother: "Jon, get your little sister's hat out of that puddle."
Jon: "I can't, she's got it strapped too tight under her chin!"

Alfie was listening to his sister practice her singing.
"Sis," he said, "I wish you'd sing Christmas carols."
"That's nice of you, Alfie," she replied. "Why?"
"Then I'd only have to hear you once a year!"

Little Brother: "I'm going to buy a sea horse."
Big Brother: "Why?"
Little Brother: "So I can play water polo!"

Rrrrrrhymes

Billy's silly, the silly Billy
He fell out of a tree
What made you so silly Billy?
I got stung by a bee!

I never saw a purple cow
I never hope to see one
But I can tell you anyhow
I'd rather see than be one!

All God's rabbits share
one bad habit
If you grow a carrot
they'll sneak up and
grab it
They dig up your turnip,
parsnip and spuds
Eat all the good ones and
leave you the duds!

A woodlouse declared his love for a mouse
But the mouse was not convinced
She ran off with a millipede
And he hasn't seen her since!

My Mum puts flies in currant pies
And mouse poop on my bread
She fries my eggs in horses' snot
And brings them up to bed!

I went to the pictures tomorrow
And took a front seat at the back
I fell from the floor to the ceiling
And broke a front bone in my back
They rushed me to hospital slowly
And starved me with plenty to eat
And when I woke up in the morning
I found I was still fast asleep!

Mary had a little lamb
She tied it to a pylon
100 volts went up its leg
And turned its wool to nylon.

If you see a Dragon
Sitting in a boat
Scare that little Dragon
By saying her boat won't float!

Pranktastic!

Here is a selection of our favourite pranks. There are some old classics in there as well as a few new ones. All these pranks are fun and safe .... just don't blame us if you get into trouble!

Don't Cry Over Spilt Milk

Tell a friend that you know a great trick. Put your hand palm-down on the table and balance a full glass of milk on the back of your hand. Bet your friend that they can't balance a glass on both hands at once (with your help to put them in place). As soon as you have the glasses balanced, get up and walk out. They will be trapped and will have to spill the milk to escape.

Classic Coin

Superglue a coin to the pavement outside your house, then watch from the window as people try to pick it up.

Confetti Shower

Put some confetti into your mum's umbrella, close it and then wait for a rainy day for her to open it.

Lazy Days

While your family sleeps, reset all the clocks ahead two hours. When they wake up they will panic and think they slept late.

Top Gloss-tip

Find an old bottle of nail polish that isn't used anymore. Unscrew the cap and set it sideways on a piece of waxed paper, letting the contents flow out into a puddle. When it dries completely, peel it off of the paper. Now you can put it anywhere and trick someone into thinking there is spilled nail polish.

Cereal-ously Frustrating

Take all the boxes of cereal in the house, remove the plastic bags containing the cereal from the boxes and switch them around. When the victim goes to eat breakfast they will do a double-take when the wrong cereal pours out.

"I love them" - Hardy Har

Going Mobile
Take your friend's mobile phone and tape it under a chair, a desk, or hide it somewhere safe and then call the number. Watch them try to find the phone, trying not to laugh of course.

Mousey Mousey
Place a sticky note underneath someone's computer mouse - ensure that it covers the ball or the optical sensor on the bottom. When they go to use the mouse, it won't work! On the post-it note write 'Got you!'

Boomph!
Open a bedroom door or any door that you know a lot of people will walk through and put a pillow at the top of it. When the person opens the door the pillow will hit them on the head.

Lost in Waste
Unroll a toilet roll several times and write: "Help, I'm lost in a toilet paper factory," on one sheet. Whoever goes to the toilet next will get a surprise.

What a Washout
Wait until your victim is in the kitchen. Go in and start filling a bucket with water (tell them you're washing the car or something). Only instead of actually filling the bucket, just pretend. Lift the bucket with both hands, acting like it's heavy and filled with water. Take a couple of steps in the victim's direction and suddenly "trip" and aim the bucket right toward them. They'll duck thinking they're getting splashed!

School Daze
Right before class, as you are walking into the classroom, ask one of your classmates if they are "ready for the test today?" This will work best if you have another friend who confirms that there is indeed a test that day. Then watch them freak out!

Crazy Crossword

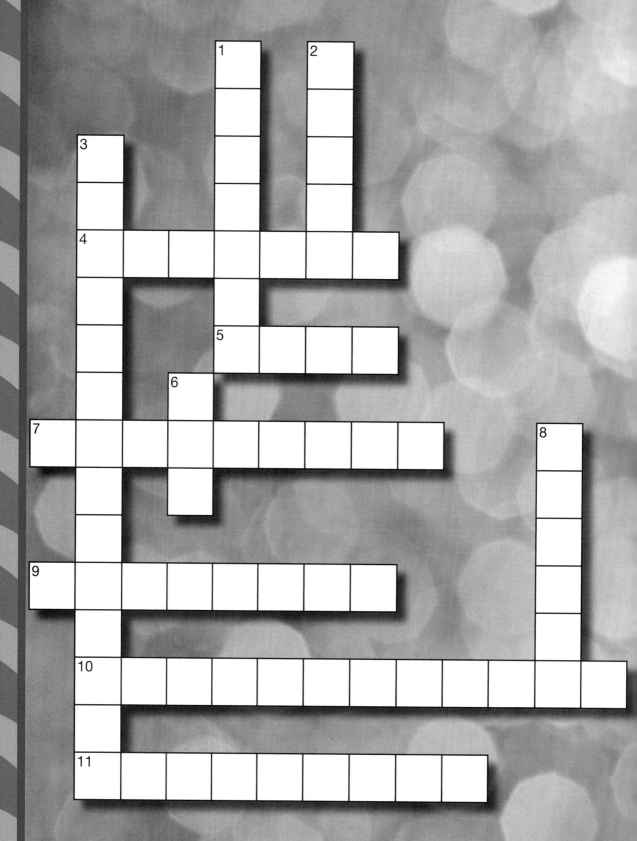

ACROSS

4 What do you call a man with a rubber toe? (7)

5 What do you call a girl with a frog on her head? (4)

7 What do you get if you cross a flea with a rabbit? (4, 5)

9 What do you get when you cross a sheep with a bee? (8)

10 What do cats eat for breakfast? (4, 8)

11 What do you call a deer with no eyes? (2, 3, 4)

DOWN

1 What do you call a man who walks through the autumn leaves? (7)

2 What do you call a man with a kilt on his head? (5)

3 What do you do when you see a spaceman? (4, 4, 3, 3)

6 What do you call a fish with no eyes? (3)

8 What do you call a man with some cat scratches on his head? (6)

Answers on page 60.

Doctor Doctor!

Patient: Doctor Doctor! I can't get to sleep.

Doctor: Lie on the edge of the bed and you'll soon drop off!

Patient: Doctor Doctor! I feel like a king.
Doctor: What's your name?
Patient: Joe.
Doctor: You must be Joe King!

Patient: Doctor Doctor! I feel so tired. I don't know where I am half the time.
Dentist: Open wide now!

Patient: Doctor Doctor! I keep losing my memory.
Doctor: When did you first notice that?
Patient: When did I first notice what?

Patient: Doctor Doctor! I think I'm a spoon.
Doctor: Sit over there please, and don't stir!

Patient: Doctor Doctor! I keep thinking there's two of me.
Doctor: One at a time please!

Patient: Doctor Doctor, everyone says I'm invisible.
Doctor: Who said that?

Patient: Doctor Doctor! I feel like a bee!
Doctor: Buzz off!

Patient: Doctor Doctor! I'm going to die in 51 seconds!

Doctor: I will be with you in a minute!

Patient: Doctor Doctor! I think I'm a goat!

Doctor: How long have you felt like this?"

Patient: Since I was a kid!

Patient: Doctor Doctor! I feel like a pack of cards.

Doctor: I'll deal with you later!

Patient: Doctor Doctor! I keep thinking I'm a bridge.

Doctor: What's come over you?

Patient: So far, three cars, a bus and a motorcycle!

Patient: Doctor Doctor! I feel like a bell!

Doctor: Don't worry, try this medicine and if it doesn't work then give me a ring!

Patient: Doctor Doctor! I feel like a pair of curtains.

Doctor: Pull yourself together!

Patient: Doctor Doctor! Everyone keeps ignoring me!

Doctor: Next please!

25

Food Funnies

What is black, white, green and bumpy?
- A pickle wearing a tuxedo.

What's the best thing to put into a pie?
- Your teeth!

"Waiter! Waiter! This food tastes kind of funny!"
- "Then why aren't you laughing?"

Why do the French like to eat snails?
- Because they don't like fast food!

What did the baby corn say to it's Mum?
- "Where is Pop corn?"

Why did the banana go to the doctor?
- Because it wasn't peeling well!

"Waiter! Waiter! Will my pizza be long?"
- "No sir, it will be round!"

What is white, has a horn, and gives milk?"
- A dairy truck!

Why don't you starve in a desert?
- Because of all the 'sand which is' there.

Food Funnies

In which school do you learn to make ice cream?
- Sunday School.

What are twin's favourite fruit?
- Pears!

What kind of keys to kids like?
- Cookies!

What do you give to a sick lemon?
- Lemon aid!

What do you call a peanut in a spacesuit?
- An astronut!

Why did the lady love to drink hot chocolate?
- Because she was a cocoa nut!

Cheese section....

Why did the cheese lose a fight with a stone?
- Because the ROQUEFORT back

What do you call cheese that isn't yours?
- NACHO CHEESE

How do you handle a dangerous cheese?
- CAERPHILLY

What kind of cheese protects a castle?
- MOAT-ZERELLA

What is a cannibal's favourite cheese?
- LIMBURGER

What cheeses do you eat on a windy day?
- BRIES

What did the cheese say to itself in the mirror?
- HALLOU-MI

What kind of cheese gets a bear out the woods?
- CAM-EM-BERT

What kind of cheese hides a horse?
- MASCARPONE

What cheese is made backwards?
- EDAM

What is a pirate's favourite cheese?
- CHEDDAAAARRRRR

That's so cheesy!

Riddle Me This

★ ★ ★ ★ ★ ★ ★ ★ ★ ★ ★ ★ ★ ★ ★ ★ ★ ★

1. I have a head and a tail, but no body. I am not a snake, what am I?

2. What house weighs the least?

3. What has arms and legs but no head?

4. The more it dries the wetter it gets. What is it?

5. What is Rupert the Bear's middle name?

6. You go in one hole, come out of three holes and when you're inside, you're ready to go outside. What is it?

1. A coin 2. A lighthouse 3. A chair 4. A towel 5. The 6. A jumper.

Riddle Me This

1. The more you take away, the bigger it gets. What is it?

2. What has no beginning, no end, and nothing in the middle?

3. If you drop a white hat into the Red Sea, what will it become?

4. Which months have 28 days?

5. It's not big but small. It sticks in the corner and doesn't move, yet it travels the world. What is it?

6. If a red house was made out of red bricks, and a blue house was made out of blue bricks, what is a green house made out of?

1. A hole   2. A doughnut   3. Wet   4. All of them do   5. A stamp   6. Glass

Animal Ha Ha

What's the difference between an injured lion and a wet day?

One pours with rain, the other roars with pain!

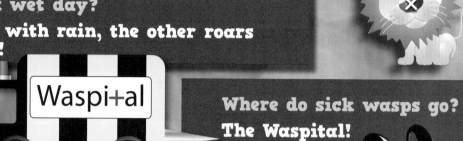

Waspi+al

Where do sick wasps go?

The Waspital!

Why do dogs run in circles?

Because it's hard to run in squares!

What happened to the cat that swallowed a ball of wool?

She had mittens!

What do you call an elephant in a phone box?

Stuck!

What do you get when you cross a porcupine with a balloon?

POP!

Where do hamsters come from?

Hamsterdam!

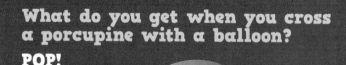

What kind of snake is good at math?

An adder!

Animal Ha Ha

What's grey and squirts jam at you?
A mouse eating a doughnut!

Why aren't elephants allowed on beaches?
They can't keep their trunks up!

What has six eyes but cannot see?
Three blind mice!

What did the clean dog say to the insect?
"Long time no flea!"

What do you call a gorilla wearing ear-muffs?
Anything you like! He can't hear you!

What's a teddy bear's favourite pasta?
Tagliateddy!

What did the frog order from the drive-thru?
Fries and a croak!

What animal would you like to be on a cold day?
A little otter!

Answers on page 60.

32

SPOT THE DIFFERENCE

Can you help Mr.Confuddled to find the 6 differences between the two photographs?

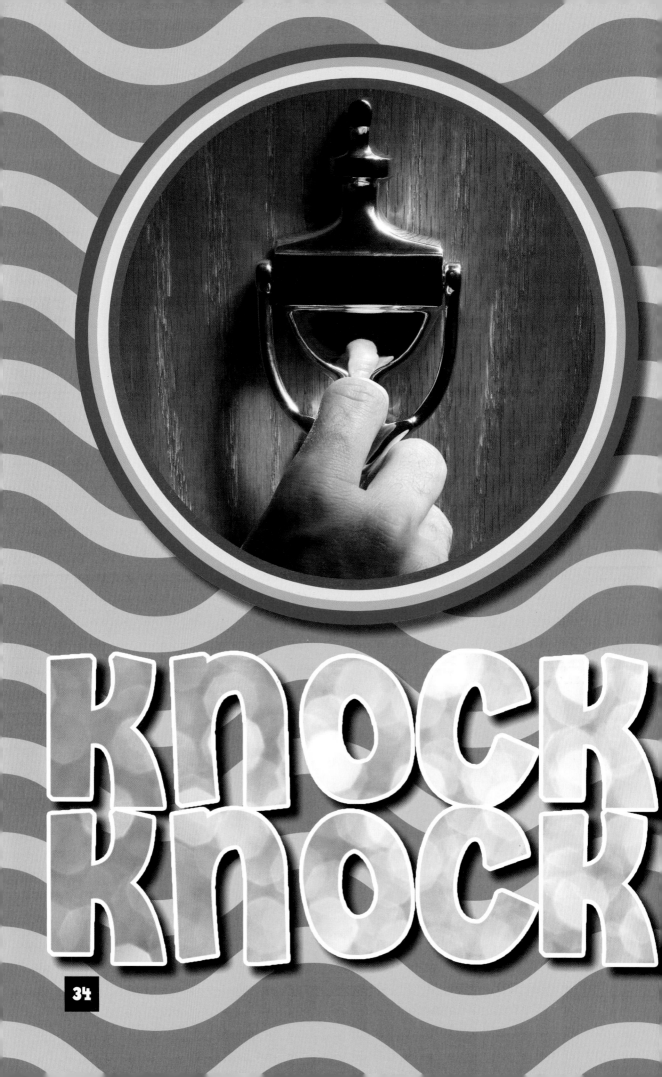

KNOCK KNOCK

Knock Knock
Who's there?
Nana!
Nana who?
Nana your business!

Knock Knock
Who's there?
Little old lady!
Little old lady who?
I didn't know you could yodel!

Knock Knock
Who's there?
Pears!
Pears who?
Pears the party!

Knock Knock
Who's there?
Quack!
Quack who?
Quack another bad joke and I'm leaving!

Knock Knock
Who's there?
Radio!
Radio who?
Radio not, here I come!

Knock Knock
Who's there?
Sam & Janet!
Sam & Janet who?
Sam & Janet evening, you will meet a stranger...!

Knock Knock
Who's there?
Tank!
Tank who?
You're welcome!

Knock Knock
Who's there?
Urinal!
Urinal who?
Urinal lot of trouble!

Knock Knock
Who's there?
Violet!
Violet who?
Violet the cat out of the bag!

Knock Knock
Who's there?
Waddle!
Waddle who?
Waddle you give me if I go away?

Knock Knock
Who's there?
X!
X who?
X-tremely pleased to meet you!

Knock Knock
Who's there?
Yvonne!
Yvonne who?
Yvonne to be alone!

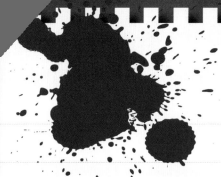

Why did the teacher wear sunglasses?
Because his class was so bright!

Have you heard about the teacher who was cross-eyed?
She couldn't control her pupils!

Teacher: Name two days of the week that start with T?
Pupil: Today and Tomorrow!

Why did the music teacher need a ladder?
To reach the high notes!

School
Rules

Teacher: James, where is your homework?
Pupil: I ate it.
Teacher: Why?
Pupil: You said it was a piece of cake!

What do elves learn in school?
The elf-abet!

Teacher: I see you missed the first day of school.
Pupil: Yes, but I didn't miss it much!

What object is king of the classroom?
The ruler!

Teacher: You've got your shoes on the wrong feet.
Pupil: But these are the only feet I've got!

SILLIES

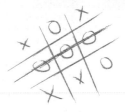

What's the difference between a teacher and a steam train?
The first goes, "Spit out that chewing gum immediately!" and the second goes, "chew chew"!

Parent: What did you learn in school today?
Kid: Not enough, I have to go back tomorrow!

Teacher: Could you please pay a little attention?
Pupil: I'm paying as little attention as I can Miss.

What is white when it's dirty and black when its clean?
A blackboard!

Why did the kid study in the airplane?
Because he wanted a higher education!

Teacher: Why are you late?
Pupil: Because of the sign.
Teacher: What sign?
Pupil: The one that says, 'School Ahead, Go Slowly.'

What did the pencil sharpener say to the pencil?
Stop going round in circles and get to the point!

CARTOON ANAG

1. Thee Who Pinion = ...

2. Brass min top = ...

3. Tadpole error hex = ...

4. Obsequent snob
   gaps par = ...

Hi, I'm Hardy Har. I have got all mixed up with some cartoon character names. Help me solve the anagrams to find out what the names are.

38

CHARACTER
~~~RAMS~~~

5. Coo so body = ...

6. Gap peppi = ...

7. Heroical & all = ...

8. Air bogey = ...

9. Lol they kit = ...

10. Pug in = ...

11. Wit when so = ...

12. Prime sand = ...

13. Razzle hit bugy = ...

14. Sons fin rap ice = ...

Answers on page 60.

Wacky Wordsearch

```
W X T T Q N O N S E N S E H
N P T E E H E E N H L X P M
B R C R C B P Q Y Y J I V Y
K K F D K V F P T S N E M H
C W R U C K M E P T P N S S
A T C V N T A J S E G B C T
R L H Z Z R O R E R N T N Y
C P E M S K E E N I Y W X C
E E E B E K P P L C M K G T
S L K R N O F T R A N K W V
I K Y O O L C N J L B L J P
W C B W N L R T N K J W V Y
M I Q T Y D E M O C Y O H G
B T J B R U O M U H N H Z D
```

Answers on page 41.

All of the words from the list are mixed up in the wordsearch below. The words can go horizontally, vertically or diagonally in any direction.

Bonkers

Cheeky

Comedy

Fun

Howl

Humour

Hysterical

Jest

Joker

Nonsense

Smile

Tears

Teehee

Tickle

Wisecrack

Woopee

I hope it's only the words that are getting scrambled up today!

Pranktastic!

Yowsa! Here are some more cheeky old and new pranks for you to play on your family and friends. Now remember......no blaming us now.

Tangled
Take the top sheet off the victim's bed, tuck the bottom of the sheet under the top end of the mattress. Pull it down and then fold it back up so that the other end is where it would be if the bed was made normally (just by the pillow). Put the pillow, blanket, etc back and make up the bed like it was before. When the victim gets into bed, they'll be surprised when they can't slide their feet all the way down to the bottom of the bed!

Bottoms up!
Place a piece of bubblewrap under the toilet seat (make sure it is hidden) so when your friend sits down, they will be surprised by a loud POP!

Toe Tugger
Stuff some cotton into the toes of your friend's shoes. They will think their feet have grown or their shoes have shrunk.

Got Ya
Point at your friend's chest acting like they have a spot on their shirt. When they look down, bring your finger up and flick their nose.

Mirror Mirror
If the person you are pranking uses a small wall mirror, take a picture facing directly away from the mirror. Crop it on your computer to exactly the same thing you would see in the mirror. Print it out on a large piece of paper, and then tape it to the mirror. Watch as the person frantically tries to see themselves.

Auto-matic
Put a note on your Mum's car that says 'Sorry about the dent. Call me so we can swap insurance

Mary had a bionic cow,
It lived on safety pins.
And every time she milked that cow
The milk came out in tins.

As I was
coming down
the stairs I met
a boy who
wasn't there.
He wasn't there
again today
I wish that boy
would go away!

If bees make jars of honey
Do wasps make jars of jam?
Did earwigs make my Marmite?
I'd better ask my nan.

I eat my peas with honey
I've done it all my life
It makes them taste quite funny
But it keeps them on the knife!

Crazy Crossword

ACROSS

1 What did 0 say to 8? (4, 4)

5 What did the Teddy bear say after he ate his dinner? (1, 2, 7)

8 What did the mountain climber name his son? (5)

9 What did the nut say when it sneezed? (6)

10 What did the mother buffalo say to her son when he left for school? (3, 3)

DOWN

2 What did one shark say to the other whilst eating a clownfish? (4, 6, 5)

3 What did the cobbler say when a cat wandered into his shop? (4)

4 What did Cinderella Dolphin wear to the ball? (5, 8)

6 What did one crisp say to the other? (5, 1, 3)

7 What did the Spanish farmer say to his chickens? (3)

Answers on page 61.

Doctor Doctor!

Patient: Doctor Doctor! I keep thinking I'm a cowboy. How long will this last?

Doctor: Usually only about a yeeeeehhhaaaaaa!

Patient: Doctor Doctor! I've a strawberry stuck in my ear!

Doctor: Don't worry, I have some cream for that!

Patient: Doctor Doctor! I think I need glasses?

Waiter: You certainly do - this is a restaurant!

Patient: Doctor Doctor! My hair is falling out. Can you give me something to keep it in?

Doctor: Certainly. How about this paper bag?

Patient: Doctor Doctor! My husband smells like fish.

Doctor: Poor sole!

Patient: Doctor Doctor! I've got wind! Can you give me something?

Doctor: Yes - here's a kite!

Patient: Doctor Doctor! I think I'm addicted to butter?

Doctor: Hmmm, this seems to be spreading!

Patient: Doctor Doctor! You have to help me out!

Doctor: Certainly, which way did you come in?

Patient: Doctor Doctor! Everyone keeps throwing me in the garbage.

Doctor: Don't talk rubbish!

Patient: Doctor Doctor! My little boy has just swallowed a roll of film.

Doctor: Well let's just wait and see if anything develops!

Patient: Doctor Doctor! I've got bad teeth, foul breath and smelly feet.

Doctor: Sounds like you've got Foot and Mouth disease!

Patient: Doctor Doctor! I think I'm suffering from Deja Vu!

Doctor: Didn't I see you yesterday?

Patient: Doctor Doctor! I feel like a pony!

Doctor: That's OK! You're just a little hoarse!

Patient: Doctor Doctor! When I press with my finger here... it hurts, and here... it hurts, and here... and here... What do you think is wrong with me?

Doctor: You have a broken finger!

Patient: Doctor Doctor! I don't feel so good! I've just eaten a red ball, a blue ball and a yellow ball.

Doctor: No wonder you aren't feeling well. You haven't been eating enough greens.

51

Riddle Me This

★★★★★★★★★★★★★★★★★★★

1. What has a face but cannot talk?

2. What has one eye but cannot see?

3. What starts with a T, ends with a T, and is full of T?

4. Which weighs more, a ton of feathers or a ton of bricks?

5. When does a cart come before a horse?

6. The turtle took two chocolates to Texas to teach Thomas to tie his boots. How many T's in that?

1. A clock 2. A needle 3. Teapot
4. None, both are a ton 5. In the Dictionary
6. Two (That)

Riddle Me This

★★★★★★★★★★★★★★★★★★

1. What goes up, but never comes down?

2. What starts with a P and ends with an E and has a million letters in it?

3. David's father had three sons: Snap, Crackle, and?

4. If you were in a race and passed the person in 2nd place, what place would you be in?

5. What two things can't you have for dinner?

6. What can a whole apple do that half an apple can't?

6. Look round
4. 2nd place   5. Breakfast and lunch
1. Your age   2. Post Office   3. David

Easter Giggles

What do you get if you pour hot water down a rabbit hole?
Hot cross bunnies!

How does the Easter Bunny stay fit?
EGG-xercise and HARE-robics!

Why did the Easter egg hide?
He was a little chicken!

How many Easter eggs can you put in an empty basket?
Only one – after that it's not empty any more!

Why shouldn't you tell an Easter egg a joke?
It might crack up!

How can you tell where the Easter Bunny has been?
Eggs (X) marks the spot!

How did the Easter Bunny rate the Easter parade?
He said it was eggs-cellent!

What's the best way to send a letter to the Easter Bunny?
Hare mail!

Why does the Easter Bunny have a shiny nose?
Because the powder puff is on the other end!

How does the Easter Bunny travel?
By hare plane!

How does the Easter Bunny keep his fur neat?
With a hare brush!

What did the rabbit say to the carrot?
It's been nice gnawing you!

How do you know carrots are good for your eyes?
Have you ever seen a rabbit wearing glasses?

How did the soggy Easter Bunny dry himself?
With a hare-dryer!

What did the rabbits do after their wedding?
Went on their bunnymoon!

What happened when the Easter Bunny met the rabbit of his dreams?
They lived hoppily ever after!

Why did the Easter Bunny cross the road?
Because the chicken had his Easter eggs!

Halloween Howlers

Who was the most famous French skeleton?
Napoleon bone-apart.

Which building does Dracula visit in New York?
The Vampire State Building.

Where do most werewolves live?
In Howllywood.

Where do most goblins live?
In North and South Scarolina.

Where does a ghost refuel his Porsche?
At a ghastly station.

What do Italians eat on Halloween?
Fettucinni Afraid-o.

What do witches use in their hair?
Scare-spray.

What do you call a little monsters parents?
Mummy and Deady.

What do you get when you cross a vampire with the internet?
Blood-thirsty hacker baby.

What do you get when you cross a pumpkin with a squash?
A squashed pumpkin pie.

Why do ghosts shiver and moan?
Because it's drafty under that sheet.

Why couldn't the mummy answer the phone?
Because he was all wrapped up!

How do vampires invite each other out for lunch?
"Do you want to go for a bite?"

Why didn't the skeleton cross the road?
Because he didn't have any guts!

Why did the witches cancel their baseball game?
Because they ran out of bats!

Christmas Crackers

What's white and goes up?
A confused snowflake!

What do you call an old snowman?
Water!

What do you sing at a snowman's birthday party?
Freeze a jolly good fellow!

Why does Santa have three gardens?
So he can ho ho ho!

Why is it always cold at Christmas?
Because it's in Decembrrrr!

Who hides in the bakery at Christmas?
A mince spy!

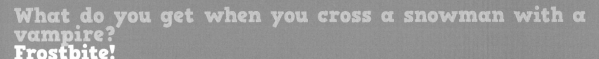

What do snowmen eat for breakfast?
Frosted flakes!

What do you get when you cross a snowman with a vampire?
Frostbite!

Where do snowmen go to dance?
A snow ball!

What do you get if you eat Christmas decorations?
Tinselitus!

How does Good King Wenceslas like his pizzas?
Deep and crisp and even!

What do monkeys sing at Christmas?
Jungle bells, jungle bells!

What do you get if you cross Santa Claus with a detective?
Santa Clues!

How do sheep greet each other at Christmas?
A merry Christmas to ewe!

What often falls at the North Pole but never gets hurt?
Snow!

What is the best Christmas present in the world?
A broken drum – you can't beat it!

Answers

Page 8, Spot The Difference

Page 14, Wacky Wordsearch

Page 22, Crazy Crossword

		R		S	
		U		C	
P		S		O	
A	R	O	B	E	R	T	O
R		L		T	
K		L	I	L	Y	
Y	F				
O	S				
B	U	G	S	B	U	N	N	Y
U	H				C
R					L
C					A
B	A	H	U	M	B	U	G
A					U
M	I	C	E	K	R	I	S	P	I	E	S
A					D
N	O	E	Y	E	D	E	E	R

Page 32, Spot The Difference

Page 38, Cartoon Anagrams

1. Winnie The Pooh
2. Bart Simpson
3. Dora The Explorer
4. Spongebob Squarepants
5. Scooby Doo
6. Peppa Pig
7. Charlie & Lola
8. Yogi Bear
9. Hello Kitty
10. Pingu
11. Snow White
12. Spiderman
13. Buzz Lightyear
14. Princess Fiona

Answers

Page 40, Wacky Wordsearch

Page 48, Crazy Crossword

We've lost Hardy Har! Can you help us find him?